A publication distributed by Heron Books

An
Anthology
of Love

An Antholog

Distribut
HERON BOO

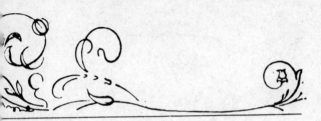

f Love

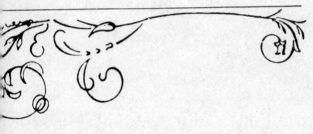

*This book
is a production of
Heron Books, London*

*Printed and bound in England by
Hazell Watson and Viney Ltd,
Aylesbury, Bucks*

2661

PREFACE

Love is an everyday thing. It is all around us. The use of the word is prostituted. But despite its universality and the fact that in one form or another it is a common experience of every one of us, it remains the inspiration par excellence for poets and writers of all complexions and all degrees of superficiality or profundity. Whether their response is comic or tragic, witty or pretty, sly or mighty, there is no other subject so generally thought about or written about. As long as the sun rises and sets, men and women will write about love.

In this anthology we hope we have gathered together a representative selection of the grand and the frivolous, from the sublimity of Donne to the playfulness of Oscar Wilde, from the passion of the Brownings to the skilled sophistication of Sidney, the flat, the sharp and the natural.

No anthology can be anything but a strange creature. It cannot but miss out more than it includes and it is bound to offend as well as please. But within these few pages there are to be found old masters and novices, and between them we trust there will be something for all tastes.

J.W.

LOVE'S SECRET

Never seek to tell thy love,
Love that never told can be;
For the gentle wind doth move
Silently, invisibly.
I told my love, I told my love,
I told her all my heart,
Trembling, cold, in ghastly fears.
Ah! She did depart!
Soon after she was gone from me,
A traveller came by,
Silently, invisibly:
He took her with a sigh.

William Blake

PROSPER MERIMEE TO AN
UNKNOWN

AS your epistle is not very amiable—excuse my frank-
ness—it has contributed somewhat to keep me in a
sullen mood. I wanted to reply to you on Sunday,
immediately and dryly. Immediately, because you
had indirectly made a sort of reproach to me; and
dryly, because I was furious against you. I was disturbed at the first word of my letter, and this distur-
bance prevented me from writing to you. Thank the
good Lord for this, for the weather is fine to-day; my
humour has become so much softened that I do not
wish to write to you any more save in a state of honey
and sugar. I shall not quarrel with you, therefore,
about twenty or thirty passages of your last letter,
which shocked me greatly, and which I am willing to
forget. I forgive you, and with the more pleasure
because, in truth, I believe I love you better when

2

you are pouting than when you are in another mood. One passage in your letter alone made me laugh for ten minutes. You say, 'short and sweet.' You say you are engaged for life as you would say, 'I am engaged for the quadrille.' Very well. Apparently I have employed my time well in disputing with you on love, marriage, and the rest; you are still at the point of believing or of saying that when one says 'Love!' one loves.... Do you know that if your love were not promised, I should think it impossible for you not to love me? How could you not love me, you that have made no promises to me, since the first law of Nature is to hold in honour whatever has the air of an obligation? And in fact, every obligation is naturally bothersome. In fine, if I had less modesty, I should consider that if you had promised your love to somebody, you will give it to me, because you have promised me nothing.

YOU shall never fall in love with me, do not fear. The consoling predictions which you make to me cannot be realised. The chances of death for me have increased this year. . . . You are an angel and a demon, but more a demon than an angel. You call me tempter. Dare to say that this word does not fit you better than me. Have you not thrown a bait to me, poor little fish; then, now that you have me at the end of your hook, you make me dance between the sky and the water as long as you please? When you are tired of the game, you will cut the thread; then the hook will be in my mouth, and I shall not be able to find the fisherman. Adieu! I promise not to fall in love with you ever. I do not want to be in love, but I should like to have a feminine friend. Pity me, for I am very sad and have a thousand reasons to be sad.

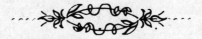

FAIN WOULD I CHANGE THAT NOTE

Fain would I change that note
　　To which fond Love hath charm'd me,
Long, long to sing by wrote,
　　Fancying that that harm'd me.
Yet when this thought doth come,
"Love is the perfect sum
　　Of all delight,"
I have no other choice
Either for pen or voice,
　　To sing or write.

O Love! they wrong thee much
　　That say thy sweet is bitter;
When they ripe fruit is such
　　As nothing can be sweeter.
Fair house of joy and bliss
Where truest pleasure is,
　　I do adore thee:
I know thee what thou art,
I serve thee with my heart
　　And fall before thee.

　　　　　　　　　　　　Anon.

SONG

Why so pale and wan, fond Lover?
Prithee why so pale?
Will, when looking well can't move her,
Looking ill prevail;
Prithee why so pale?

Why so dull and mute young Sinner?
Prithee why so mute?
Will, when speaking well can't win her,
Saying nothing do't:
Prithee why so mute?

Quit, quit for shame, this will not move,
This cannot take her;
If of herself she will not love,
Nothing can make her:
The Devil take her.

Sir John Suckling

Take all my loves, my love, yea, take them all;
What hast thou then more than thou hadst before?
No love, my love, that thou mayst true love call;
All mine was thine before thou hadst this more.
Then if for my love thou my love receivest,
I cannot blame thee, for my love thou usest;
But yet be blam'd, if thou thyself deceivest
By wilful taste of what thyself refusest.
I do forgive thy robb'ry, gentle thief,
Although thou steal thee all my poverty;
And yet love knows it is a greater grief
To bear love's wrong than hate's known injury.
  Lascivious grace, in whom all ill well shows,
    Kill me with spites; yet we must not be foes.

William Shakespeare

JACOB ORTIS TO AN UNKNOWN

I SAY within myself—'And is it indeed true, that this angel of heaven exists here, in this nether world—among us?' For I suspect that I have become enamoured of the creature of my own fancy.

But who would not have desired to love her, even though unhappily? and where is the happy man with whom I would deign to exchange my present deplorable state? . . . but who can I, on the other hand, be so much my own enemy as to torment myself, Heaven knows! without any hope whatever? A certain pride, perhaps of this girl, both in her own beauty and my misfortunes . . . she does not love me; and her pity may hatch a treachery. But that celestial kiss of hers which is ever on my lips, and which governs all my thoughts, and those tears!

. . . Alas! ever since that moment she avoids me; nor dare she any longer look me in the face. A seducer!—I? Oh when I hear that tremendous sentence thunder in my soul, 'I never shall be yours,' I pass from rage to madness, and meditate crimes of blood. . . . Not thou, heavenly girl! I, I alone, have attempted treachery. . . .

Oh! one other kiss of thine, and abandon me afterwards to my dreams, and sweet delirium.

I shall die at thy feet; but wholly thine—wholly. Thou, if thou canst not be my wife, shall be, at least, my companion in the grave. Ah no! let the punishment of this fatal love be poured down upon me alone. Let me mourn to all eternity; but may heaven never, oh Teresa! make thee through me unhappy. But I, in the meantime, have lost thee, and thou thyself fliest from me. Ah! didst thou love me as I love thee . . .

Nevertheless, oh Lorenzo! amidst doubts so cruel, amidst so many torments, every time that I ask counsel from reason, she comforts me by saying— *Thou art not immortal.* Away! let me suffer then; and even to the utmost. I shall go forth from the hell of life; and I alone suffice. With this idea I laugh to scorn both fortune and man.

My letters! all dead paper, mute and white!
And yet they seem alive and quivering
Against my tremulous hands which loose the string
And let them drop down on my knee tonight.
This said, - he wished to have me in his sight
Once, as a friend: this fixed a day in spring
To come and touch my hand . . . a simple thing,
Yet I wept for it! - this, . . . the paper's light . . .
Said, Dear, I love thee; and I sank and quailed
As if God's future thundered on my past.
This said, I am thine - and so its ink has paled
With lying at my heart that beat too fast.
And this . . . O love, thy words have ill availed
If, what this said, I dared repeat at last!

Elizabeth Barrett Browning

How do I love thee? Let me count the ways.
I love thee to the depth and breadth and height
My soul can reach, when feeling out of sight
For the ends of Being and ideal Grace.
I love thee to the level of everyday's
Most quiet need, by sun and candle-light.
I love thee freely, as men strive for Right;
I love thee purely, as they turn from Praise.
I love thee with the passion put to use
In my old griefs, and with my childhood's faith.
I love thee with a love I seemed to lose
With my lost saints, - I love thee with the breath,
Smiles, tears of all my life! - and, if God choose,
I shall but love thee better after death.

Elizabeth Barrett Browning

THOU knowest my heart; thou knowest that all there is desire, thought, boding and longing; thou livest among spirits, and they give thee divine wisdom. Thou must nourish me; thou givest all that in advance which I do not understand to ask for. My mind has a small embrace, my love a large one; thou must bring them to a balance. Love cannot be quiet till the mind matches its growth; thou art matched to my love; thou are friendly, kind, indulgent; let me know when my heart is off the balance. I understand thy silent signs.

A look from thy eyes into mine, a kiss from thee upon my lips, instructs me in all, what might seem delightful to learn, to one who, like me, had experience from those. I am far from thee; mine are become strange to me. I must ever return in thought to that hour, when thou holdest me in the soft fold of thy arm. Then I begin to weep, but the tears dry again unawares. Yes, he reaches with his love (thus I think) over to me in this concealed stillness; and should not I, with my eternal undisturbed longing, reach to him in the distance? Ah, conceive what my heart has to say to thee; it overflows with soft sighs, all whisper to thee. Be my only happiness on earth thy friendly will to me. O, dear friend! give me but a sign that thou are conscious of me.

GOETHE TO BETTINE BRENTANO

WHAT can one say and give to thee, which is not already in a more beautiful way become thine own? One must be silent and give thee thy way. When an opportunity offers to beg something of thee, then, one may let his thanks for the much which has unexpectedly been given through the riches of thy love, flow in the same stream. That thou cherishest my mother, I would fain with my whole heart requite thee; from yonder a sharp breeze blew upon me, and now that I know that thou art with her, I feel safe and warm.

I do not say to thee 'come,' I will not have the little bird disturbed from its nest; but the accident would not be unwelcome to me, which should make use of storm and tempest to bring it safely beneath my roof. At any rate, Dearest Bettine, remember that thou art on the road to spoil me.

GOETHE.

BOLDNESS IN LOVE

Mark how the bashful morn in vain
Courts the amorous marigold,
With sighing blasts and weeping rain,
Yet she refuses to unfold.
But when the planet of the day
Approacheth with his powerful ray,
Then she spreads, then she receives
His warmer beams into her virgin leaves.

So shalt thou thrive in love, fond boy;
If thy tears and sighs discover
Thy grief, thou never shalt enjoy
The just reward of a bold lover.
But when with moving accents thou
Shalt constant faith and service vow,
Thy Celia shall receive those charms
With open ears, and with unfolded arms.

Thomas Carew

15

"IS LOVE A FANCY"

Is love a fancy, or a feeling? No,
It is immortal as immaculate Truth.
'Tis not a blossom, shed as soon as youth
Drops from the stem of life—for it will grow
In barren regions, where no waters flow,
Nor ray of promise cheats the pensive gloom.
A darkling fire, faint hovering o'er a tomb,
That but itself and darkness nought doth show,
Is my love's being,—yet it cannot die,
Nor will it change, though all be changed beside;
Though fairest beauty be no longer fair,
Though vows be false, and faith itself deny,
Though sharp enjoyment be a suicide,
And hope a spectre in a ruin bare.

Hartley Coleridge

A BIRTHDAY

My heart is like a singing bird
　　Whose nest is in a watered shoot;
My heart is like an apple-tree
　　Whose boughs are bent with thickset fruit;
My heart is like a rainbow shell
　　That paddles in a halcyon sea;
My heart is gladder than all these,
　　Because my love is come to me.

Raise me a dais of silk and down;
　　Hang it with vair and purple dyes;
Carve it in doves and pomegranates,
　　And peacocks with a hundred eyes;
Work it in gold and silver grapes,
　　In leaves, and silver fleurs-de-lys;
Because the birthday of my life
　　Is come, my love is come to me.

Christina Rossetti

BEAU BRUMMELL TO ONE OF
HIS CONQUESTS

YESTERDAY morning I was subdued almost to insanity, but your note in the evening restored me to peace and equanimity, and as if I had been redeemed from earthly purgatory, placed me in Heaven.

Thank you, thank you, dearest of beings; how can I retribute all this benevolent open-heartedness, the delightful proof and avowal of my not being indifferent to you? I cannot, by inanimate words represent the excess of my feelings towards you; take them with indulgent admission and forbearance, the simple boon and sacred pledge of my heart's deepest affections for you; they are rooted in my very soul and existence; they will never deviate; they will never die away. By the glimmering light that was remaining I perceived something white at your *porte cochère*. It was evident that I was recognized, and the figure advanced with your billet. In an instant I seized the hand of your faithful and intelligent messenger, compressed it forcibly, and had she been as forbidding as the old Dowager Duchess of ――― I should have saluted her, if I had not fancied at the instant that I heard someone coming up the street. We parted and I returned to my solitary chamber. There I lacerated the letter with impatience, and then the light of love and joy and the refreshing breath of evening stole through the open window over my entranced senses. After that I sought another stroll on the ramparts, and again returned home contented with you, with myself and with the world.

'I slept the slumbers of a saint forgiven.
And mild as opening dreams of promised Heaven.'

I have known few that could equal, none that could excel you; yet they possessed not your charm of countenance, your form, your heart, in my estimation. Certainly they did not possess that unaffected and fervent homage, which in my constant memory,— in my heart's life blood,—and in my devoted soul I bear to you.

Ever most affectionatley yours,
GEORGE BRUMMELL.

LA BELLE DAME SANS MERCI

'O What can ail thee, knight-at-arms,
Alone and palely loitering?
The sedge is wither'd from the lake,
And no birds sing.

O what can ail thee, knight-at-arms,
So haggard and so woe-begone?
The squirrel's granary is full,
And the harvest's done.

I see a lily on thy brow
With anguish moist and fever dew;
And on thy cheek a fading rose
Fast withereth too'.

'I met a lady in the meads,
Full beautiful - a faery's child,
Her hair was long, her foot was light,
And her eyes were wild.

I made a garland for her head,
And bracelets too, and fragrant zone;
She look'd at me as she did love,
And made sweet moan.

I set her on my pacing steed
And nothing else saw all day long,
For sideways would she lean, and sing
A faery's song.

She found me roots of relish sweet,
And honey wild and manna dew,
And sure in language strange she said,
"I love thee true!"

She took me to her elfin grot,
And there she wept and sigh'd full sore;
And there I shut her wild, wild eyes
With kisses four.

And there she lulled me asleep,
And there I dream'd - Ah! woe betide!
The latest dream I ever dream'd
On the cold hill's side.

I saw pale kings and princes too,
Pale warriors, death-pale were they all;
Who cried - La belle Dame sans Merci
Hath thee in thrall!"

I saw their starved lips in the gloam
With horrid warning gaped wide,
And I awoke and found me here
On the cold hill's side.

And this is why I sojourn here
Alone and palely loitering,
Though the sedge is wither'd from the lake,
And no birds sing'.

John Keats

A CANDLE

There is a thing which in the light
Is seldom used; but in the night
It serves the maiden female crew,
The ladies, and the good-wives too:
They use to take it in their hand,
And then it will uprightly stand;
And to a hole they it apply,
Where by its goodwill it would die;
It spends, goes out, and still within
It leaves its moisture thick and thin.

Sir John Suckling

TO MISTRESS MARGARET HUSSEY

Merry Margaret,
As midsummer flower,
Gentle as falcon
Or hawk of the tower;
With solace and gladness,
Much mirth and no madness,
All good and no badness,
So joyously,
So maidenly,
So womanly
Her demeaning
In every thing,
Far, far passing
That I can endite,
Or suffice to write
Of merry Margaret,
As midsummer flower,
Gentle as falcon
Or hawk of the tower;
as patient and as still,
And as full of good will,
As fair Ysaphill;
Coriander

Sweet pomander,
Good Cassanda;
Steadfast of thought,
Well made, well wrought;
Far may be sought
Here that you can find
So courteous, so kind
As merry Margaret,
This midsummer flower,
Gentle as falcon
Or hawk of the tower.

John Skelton

As unto the bow the cord is,
So unto the man is woman;
Though she bends him, she obeys him,
Though she draws him, yet she follows;
Useless each without the other!

LONGFELLOW, *Hiawatha's Wooing.*

LORD GREY AND LADY
HENRIETTA BERKELEY

(Sylvia to Philander)

ANOTHER night, oh heavens, and yet no letter come! Where are you, my Philander? What happy place contains you? If in heaven why does not some posting angel bid me haste after you? If on earth why does not some little god of love bring the grateful tidings on his painted wings? If sick, why does not my own fond heart by sympathy inform me? But that is all active, vigorous, wishing, impatient of delaying, silent, and busy in imagination. If you are false, if you have forgotten your poor, believing and distracted Sylvia, why does not that kind tyrant, Death, that meagre welcome vision of the despairing, old, and wretched, approach in dead of night, approach my restless bed, and toll the dismal tidings in my frighted listening ears, and strike me for ever silent, lay me for ever quiet, lost to the world, lost to my faithless charmer!

But if a sense of honour in you had made you resolve to prefer mine before your love, made you take up a noble, fatal resolution never to tell me more of your passion, this were a trial I fear my fond heart wants courage to bear; or is it a trick, a cold fit only assumed to try how much I love you? I have no arts, heaven knows, no guile or double meaning in my soul; it is all plain native simplicity, fearful and timorous as children in the night, trembling as doves pursued: born soft by nature, and made tender by love, what, oh! what will become of me then? Yet would I were confirmed in all my fears. For, as I am, my condition is yet more deplorable; for I am in doubt, and doubt is the worst torment of the mind. Oh, Philander, be merciful, and let me know the worst. Do not be cruel while you kill, do it with pity to the wretched Sylvia. Oh let me quickly know whether you are at all. Your most impatient and unfortunate Sylvia I rave, I die for some relief.

LORD GREY AND LADY
HENRIETTA BERKELEY

(Philander to Sylvia)

MY soul's eternal joy, my Sylvia! What have you done, and oh, how durst you, knowing my fond heart, try it with so fatal a stroke? What means this severe letter? and why so eagerly at this time? Woe the day! Is Myrtilla's virtue so defended? Is it a question now whether she is false or not? Oh, poor, oh frivolous excuse! You love me not; by all that's good, you love me not. To try your power you have flattered and feigned. Oh woman, false, charming woman! You have undone me, I rave, and shall commit such extravagance, that will ruin both, I must upbraid you, fickle, and inconstant, I must. And this distance will not serve, it is too great; my reproaches lose their force, I burst with resentment, with injured love, and you are either the most faithless of your sex, or the most malicious and tormenting. Oh, I am past tricks Sylvia, your little arts might do well in a beginning flame, but to a settled fire that is arrived to the highest degree, it does but damp its fierceness, and,

28

instead of drawing one on, would lessen my esteem, if any such deceit were capable to harbour in the heart of Sylvia; but she is all divine, and I am mistaken in the meaning of what she says.

Remember, oh Sylvia, that five tedious days are past since I sighed at your dear feet; and five days to a man so madly in love as your Philander, is a tedious age; it is now six o'clock in the morning, Brillard will be with you by eight, and by ten I may have permission to see you, and then I need not say how soon I will present myself before you at Belfont. For heaven's sake, my eternal blessing, if you design me this happiness, contrive it so that I may see nobody that belongs to Belfont but the fair, the lovely Sylvia; for I must be more moments with you than will be convenient to be taken notice of, lest they suspect our business to be love, and that discovery yet may ruin us. Oh, I will delay no longer, my soul is impatient to see you. I cannot live another night without it. I die, by heaven, I languish for the appointed hour. You will believe, when you see my languid face and dying eyes how much and great a sufferer I am.

My soul's delight, you may perhaps deny me from your fear, but, on, do not, though I ask a mighty blessing. Oh, though I faint with the thought only of so blessed an opportunity, yet you shall secure me, by what vows, by what imprecations, by what ties you please. But let me hear your angel's voice and have the transporting joy of throwing myself at your feet. And if you please, give me leave (a man condemned eternally to love) to plead a little for my life and passion. Let me remove your fears; and though that mighty task never make me entirely happy, at least it will be a great satisfaction to me to know that it is not through my fault that I am the

Most wretched
PHILANDER.

DIDEROT TO SOPHIE VOLAND

Au Grandval,
20th October, 1759.

YOU are well! You think of me! You love me. You will always love me. I believe you: now I am happy. I live again. I can talk, work, play, walk—do anything you wish. I must have made myself very disagreeable the last two or thee days. No! my love; your very presence would not have delighted me more than your first letter did.

How impatiently I waited for it! I am sure my hands trembled when opening it. My countenance changed; my voice altered; and unless he were a fool, he who handed it to me would have said—'That man receives news from his father or mother, or someone else he loves.' I was just at that moment about to send you a letter expressing my great uneasiness. While you are amusing yourself, you forget how much my heart suffers. . . .

Adieu, my dearest love. My affection for you is ardent and sincere. I would love you even more than I do, if I knew how.

DIDEROT TO SOPHIE VOLAND

July 1759.

I CANNOT leave this place without saying a few words to you. So, my pet, you expect a good deal from me. Your happiness, your life, even, depend, you say, upon my ever loving you!

Never fear, my dear Sophie; that will endure, and you shall live, and be happy. I have never committed a crime yet, and am not going to begin. I am wholly yours—you are everything to me; we will sustain each other in all the ills of life it may please fate to inflict upon us; you will soothe my troubles; I will comfort you in yours. Would that I could always see you as you have been lately! As for myself, you must confess that I am just as I was on the first day you saw me.

This is no merit of my own; but I owe it in justice to myself to tell you so. It is one effect of good qualities to be felt more vividly from day to day. Be assured of my constancy to yours, and of my appreciation of them. Never was a passion more justified by reason than mine. Is it not true, my dear Sophie, that you are very amiable? Examine yourself—see how worthy you are of being loved; and know that I love you very much. That is the unvarying standard of my feelings.

OUT UPON IT

Out upon it, I have loved
  Three whole days together;
And am like to love three more,
  If it prove fair weather.

Time shall moult away his wings
  Ere he shall discover
In the whole wide world again
  Such a constant Lover.

But the spite on't is, no praise
  Is due at all to me:
Love with me had made no stays
  Had it any been but she.

Had it any been but she,
  And that very Face,
There had been at least ere this
  A dozen dozen in her place.

                              Sir John Suckling

Discovering reciprocal love should really disenchant
the lover with regard to the beloved. "What! *She* is
modest enough to love even you? Or stupid enough?
Or—or."

NIETZSCHE, *Beyond Good and Evil*

One can find women who have never had one love
affair, but it is rare indeed to find any who have had
only one.

LA ROCHEFOUCAULD

There goes a saying, and 'twas shrewdly said,
Old fish at table, young flesh in bed.
My soul abhors the tasteless dry embrace
Of a stale virgin with a winter face.

ALEXANDER POPE, *January and May*

The Lion is the King of Beasts, but he is scarcely suitable for a domestic pet. In the same way, I suspect love is rather too violent a passion to make, in all cases, a good domestic sentiment.

ROBERT LOUIS STEVENSON, *Virginibus Puerisque.*

Werther had a love for Charlotte
 Such as words could never utter;
Would you know how first he met her?
 She was cutting bread and butter.

THACKERAY, *The Sorrows of Werther.*

TO HIS COY MISTRESS

Had we but World enough, and Time,
This coyness Lady were no crime.
We would sit down, and think which way
To walk, and pass our long Loves Day.
Thou by the Indian Ganges side
Should'st Rubies find: I by the Tide
Of Humber would complain. I would
Love you ten years before the Flood:
And you should if you please refuse
Till the Conversion of the Jews.
My vegetable Love should grow
Vaster then Empires, and more slow.
An hundred years should go to praise
Thine Eyes, and on thy Forehead gaze.
Two hundred to adore each Breast:
But thirty thousand to the rest.
An Age at least to every part,
And the last Age should show your Heart.
For Lady you deserve this State;
Nor would I love at lower rate.

But at my back I always hear
Times winged Chariot hurrying near:
And yonder all before us lie

Deserts of vast Eternity.
Thy Beauty shall no more be found;
Nor, in thy marble Vault, shall sound
My echoing Song: then Worms shall try
That long preserv'd Virginity:
And your quaint Honour turn to dust;
And into ashes all my Lust.
The Grave's a fine and private place,
But none I think do there embrace.
    Now therefore, while the youthful hue
Sits on thy skin like morning dew,
And while thy willing Soul transpires
At every pore with instant Fires,
Now let us sport us while we may;
And now, like amorous birds of prey,
Rather at once our Time devour,
Than languish in his slow-chapt power.
Let us roll all our Strength, and all
Our sweetness, up into one Ball:
And tear our Pleasures with rough strife,
Thorough the Iron gates of Life.
Thus, though we cannot make our Sun
Stand still, yet we will make him run.

Andrew Marvell

First time he kissed me, he but only kissed
The fingers of this hand wherewith I wrote;
And ever since, it grew more clean and white,
Slow to world-greetings, quick with its 'Oh, list',
When the angels speak. A ring of amethyst
I could not wear here, plainer to my sight,
Than that first kiss. The second, passed in height
The first, and sought the forehead, and half missed,
Half falling on the hair. O beyond meed!
That was the chrism of love, which love's own crown,
With sanctifying sweetness, did precede.
The third upon my lips was folded down
In perfect, purple state; since when, indeed,
I have been proud and said, 'My love, my own'.

Elizabeth Barrett Browning

Ham.: Is this the prologue or the posy of a ring?
Oph.: 'Tis brief, my lord.
Ham.: As woman's love.
  SHAKESPEARE, *Hamlet*.

He plough'd her, and she cropp'd.
  SHAKESPEARE, *Antony and Cleopatra*.

The success of any man with any woman is apt to displease even his best friends.
  MADAME DE STAEL

Though her [Lady Elizabeth Hastings'] mien carries much more invitation than command, to behold her is an immediate check to loose behaviour; to love her was a liberal education.
  SIR RICHARD STEELE, *The Tatler*

MARY WOLLSTONECRAFT TO
GILBERT IMLAY

Past Twelve o'clock Monday night,
Paris, *Aug. 1793.*

I OBEY an emotion of my heart, which made me think of wishing thee, my love, good-night! before I go to rest, with more tenderness than I can to-morrow, when writing a hasty line or two under Colonel ———'s eye. You can scarcely imagine with what pleasure I anticipate the day, when we are to begin almost to live together; and you would smile to hear how many plans of employment I have in my head, now that I am confident my heart has found peace in your bosom. - Cherish me with that dignified tenderness, which I have only found in you; and your own dear will try to keep under a quickness of feeling, that has sometimes given you pain. — Yes, I will be *good,* that I may deserve to be happy; and whilst you love me, I cannot again fall into the miserable state, which rendered life a burthen almost too heavy to be borne.

But, good-night! — God bless you! Sterne says, that is equal to a kiss — yet I would rather give you the kiss into the bargain, glowing with gratitude to Heaven, and affection to you. I like the word affection, because it signifies something habitual; and we are soon to meet, to try whether we have mind enough to keep our hearts warm.

MARY.

I will be at the barrier a little after ten o'clock to-morrow.—Yours—

MARY WOLLSTONECRAFT TO GILBERT IMLAY

Friday Morning, Paris, *Dec. 1793.*

I AM glad to find that other people can be unreasonable, as well as myself—for be it known to thee, that I answered thy *first* letter, the very night it reached me (Sunday), though thou couldst not receive it before Wednesday, because it was not sent off till the next day.—There is a full, true, and particular account.—

Yet I am not angry with thee, my love, for I think that it is a proof of stupidity, and likewise of a milk-and-water affection, which comes to the same thing, when the temper is governed by a square and compass.—There is nothing picturesque in this straight-lined equality, and the passions always give grace to the actions.

Recollection now makes my heart bound to thee; but, it is not to thy money-getting face, though I cannot be seriously displeased with the exertion which increases my esteem, or rather is what I should have expected from thy character.—No; I have thy honest countenance before me—Pop—relaxed by tenderness; a little—little wounded by my whims; and thy eyes glistening with sympathy.—Thy lips then feel softer than soft—and I rest my cheek on thine, forgetting all the world.—I have not left the hue of love out of the picture—the rosy glow; and fancy has spread it over my own cheeks, I believe, for I feel them burning, whilst a delicious tear trembles in my eye, that would be all your own, if a grateful emotion directed to the Father of nature, who has made me thus alive to happiness, did not give more warmth to the sentiment it divides—I must pause a moment.

Need I tell you that I am tranquil after writing thus?—I do not know why, but I have more confidence in your affection, when absent, than present; nay, I think that you must love me, for, in the sincerity of my heart let me say it, I believe I deserve

your tenderness, because I am true, and have a degree
of sensibility that you can see and relish.

Yours sincerely,
MARY.

When Love with unconfined wings
   Hovers within my gates;
And my divine Althea brings
   To whisper at the grates:
When I lie tangled in her hair,
   And fettered to her eye;
The Gods, that wanton in the air,
   Know no such liberty.

RICHARD LOVELACE, *To Althea, From Prison.*

But love, first learned in a lady's eyes,
Lives not alone immured in the brain,
But, with the motion of all elements,
Courses as swift as thought in every power,
And gives to every power a double power,
Above their functions and their offices.
It adds a precious seeing to the eye;
A lover's eyes will gaze an eagle blind;
A lover's ears will hear the lowest sound,
When the suspicious head of theft is stopp'd:
Love's feeling is more soft and sensible
Than are the tender horns of cockled snails:
Love's tongue proves dainty Bacchus gross in taste.
For valour, is not love a Hercules,
Still climbing trees in the Hesperides?
Subtle as Sphinx; as sweet and musical
As bright Apollo's lute, strung with his hair;
And when Love speaks, the voice of all the gods
Makes heaven drowsy with the harmony.
Never durst poet touch a pen to write
Until his ink were temper'd with Love's sighs.

SHAKESPEARE, *Love's Labour's Lost,*

IN A GONDOLA

The moth's kiss, first!
Kiss me as if you made believe
You were not sure, this eve,
How my face, your flower, had pursed
Its petals up; so, here and there
You brush it, till I grow aware
Who wants me, and wide ope I burst.

The bee's kiss, now!
Kiss me as if you entered gay
My heart at some noonday,
A bud that dares not disallow
The claim, so all is rendered up,
And passively its shattered cup
Over your head to sleep I bow.

Robert Browning

~~~

Those who are faithful know only the trivial side of
love: it is the faithless who know love's tragedies.
  OSCAR WILDE, *The Picture of Dorian Gray.*

THERE IS A GARDEN IN HER FACE

There is a Garden in her face,
Where Roses and white Lillies grow;
A heav'nly paradise is that place,
Wherein all pleasant fruits do flow.
There Cherries grow, which none may buy
Till Cherry ripe themselves do cry.

Those Cherries fairly do enclose
Of Orient Pearl a double row;
Which when her lovely laughter shows,
They look like Rose buds fill'd with snow.
Yet them not Peer nor Prince can buy,
Till Cherry ripe themselves do cry.

Her Eyes like Angels watch them still;
Her Brows like bended boughs do stand,
Threatening with piercing frowns to kill
All that attempt with eye or hand
Those sacred Cherries to come nigh,
Till Cherry ripe themselves do cry.

Thomas Campion

I COULD NOT THOUGH I WOULD

I could not though I would: good Lady say not so,
Since one good word of your good will might soone re-
  dresse my wo
Where would is free before, there could never fayle:
For profe, you see how gallies passe where ships can
  beare no sayle.
The weary mariner when skies are overcast,
By ready will doth guyde his skill and wins the haven
  at last.
The prety byrd that sings with pricke against hir brest,
Doth make a vertue of hir need to watch when others
  rest.
And true the proverbe is, which you have layed apart,
There is no hap can seeme to hard unto a willing hart.
Then lovely Lady myne, you say not as you should,
In doubtful termes to aunswer thus: I could not thogh
  I would.
Yes, yes, full well you know, your can is quicke and
  good:

And wilful will is e'en too swift to shed my guiltless
    blood.
But if good will were bent as pressed as power is,
Such will would quickly find the skill to mend that
    is amiss.
Wherefore if you desire to see my true love spilt,
Command and I will slay myself, that yours may be
    the guilt.
But if you have no power to say your servant nay,
Write thus: I may not as I would, yet must I as I may.

George Gascoigne

When one is in love, one always begins by deceiving
oneself, and one always ends by deceiving others.
That is what the world calls a romance.
  OSCAR WILDE, *The Picture of Dorian Gray.*

VICTOR HUGO TO ADELE
FOUCHER

January 1820.

A FEW words from you, my beloved Adèle, have again changed the state of my mind. Yes, you can do anything with me, and to-morrow, I should be dead indeed if the gentle sound of your voice, the tender pressure of your adored lips, do not suffice to recall the life to my body. With what different feelings to yesterday's I shall lay myself down to-night! Yesterday, Adèle, I no longer believed in your love; the hour of death would have been welcome to me.

And yet I still said to myself, 'if it be true that she does not love me, if nothing in me could deserve the blessing of her love, without which there is no longer any charm in life, is that a reason for dying? Do I exist for my own personal happiness? No; my whole existence is devoted to her, even in spite of her. And by what right should I have dared to aspire to her love? Am I, then, more than an angel or a deity? I love her, true, even I; I am ready to sacrifice everything gladly for her sake—everything, even the hope of being loved by her; there is no devotedness of which I am not capable for her, for one of her smiles. for one of her looks. But could I be otherwise? Is she not the sole aim of my life? That she may show indifference to me, even hate, will be my misfortune, that is all. What does it matter, so that it does not injure her happiness? Yes, if she cannot love me I ought to blame myself only. My duty is to keep close to her steps, to surround her existence with mine, to serve her as a barrier against all dangers, to offer her my head as a stepping-stone, to place myself unceasingly between her and all sorrows, without claiming any reward, without expecting any recompense. Only too happy if she deign sometimes to cast a pitying look upon her slave, and to remember him in the hour of danger! Alas! if she only allow me to give my life to anticipate her every desire, all her caprices; if she but permit me to kiss with respect her adored footprints; if she but consent to lean upon me at times amidst the difficulties of life: Then I shall have obtained the only happiness to which I have the presumption to aspire. Because I am ready to sacrifice all for her, does she owe me any gratitude? Is it her fault that I love her? Must she, on that account, believe herself constrained to love me? No! she may sport with my devotion, repay my services with hate, and repulse my idolatry with scorn, without my having for a moment the right to complain of that angel; nor ought I to cease for an instant to lavish upon her all that which she would disdain. And should every one of my days have been marked by some sacrifice for her, I should still, at the day of my death have discharged nothing of the infinite debt that my existence owes to hers.'

Such, my well-beloved Adèle, were the thoughts and resolutions of my mind at this time yesterday. To-day they are still the same. Only there is mingled with them the certainty of happiness—such great happiness that I cannot think of it without trembling, and scarcely dare to believe in it.

Then it is true that you love me, Adèle? Tell me, can I trust in this enchanting idea? Don't you think that I shall end by becoming insane with joy if ever I can pass the whole of my life at your feet, sure of making you as happy as I shall be myself, sure of being adored by you as you are adored by me? Oh! your letter has restored peace to me, your words this evening have filled me with happiness. A thousand thanks, Adèle, my well-beloved angel. Would that I could prostrate myself before you as before a divinity. How happy you make me! Adieu, adieu, I shall pass a very happy night, dreaming of you.

Sleep well, and allow your husband to take the twelve kisses which you promised him, besides all those yet unpromised.

Let me confess that we two must be twain,
Although our undivided loves are one;
So shall those blots that do with me remain,
Without thy help, by me be borne alone.
In our two loves there is but one respect,
Though in our lives a separable spite,
Which though it alter not love's sole effect,
Yet doth it steal sweet hours from love's delight.
I may not evermore acknowledge thee,
Lest my bewailed guilt should do thee shame;
Nor thou with public kindness honour me,
Unless thou take that honour from thy name.
    But do not so; I love thee in such sort
    As, thou being mine, mine is thy good report.

William Shakespeare

SONNET

Thus ends my love, but this doth grieve me most,
　　That so it ends; but that ends too; this yet,
Besides the wishes, hopes and time I lost,
　　Troubles my mind awhile, that I am set
Free, worse than deni'd: I can neither boast
　　Choice nor success, as my case is, nor get
Pardon from myself that I loved not
　　A better mistress, or her worse; this debt
Only's her due still, that she be forgot
Ere chang'd, lest I love none; this done, the taint
　　Of foul inconstancy is clear'd at least
In me, there only rests but to unpaint
　　Her form in my mind, that so dispossess'd,
It be a temple, but without a saint.

Lord Herbert

LIFE IN A LOVE

Escape me?
Never -
Beloved!
While I am I, and you are you,
So long as the world contains us both,
Me the loving and you the loth,
While the one eludes, must the other pursue.
My life is a fault at last, I fear:
It seems too much like a fate, indeed!
Though I do my best I shall scarce succeed.
But what if I fail of my purpose here?
It is but to keep the nerves at strain,
To dry one's eyes and laugh at a fall,
And, baffled, get up and begin again, -
So the chase takes up one's life, that's all.
While, look but once from your farthest bound
At me so deep in the dust and dark,
No sooner the old hope goes to ground
Than a new one, straight to the self-same mark,
I shape me -
Ever
Removed!

Robert Browning

MDLLE DE LESPINASSE TO MON.
DE GUILBERT

I have not seen you and you tell me it is not your fault! If you had the thousandth part of a wish to see me that I have to see you, you would be here, and I should be happy. No, I was mistaken, and I suffer; but I do not covet the pleasures of heaven. Dearest, I love you to distraction, to folly, to extravagance, to despair!

Every day you torture my heart most cruelly. I saw you this morning, and forgot it all; and it seemed to me as if I could not make enough of you, loving you with my whole soul, and feeling as if I could live and die for you. You deserve more than that of me; yes, if I only knew that you loved me, it would be as nothing, for nothing can be more simple and natural than to love to distraction one who is so good as you are. But dear friend, I more than love, I suffer.

I will give up all my happiness for your good. But here is some one come to disturb the satisfaction I have in proving to you how much I love you. Do you wish to know why I write to you? It is because it gives me pleasure. You need never doubt it, since I have told you so. But where are you? If you are happy I must not complain at your leaving me miserable.

MDLLE DE LESPINASSE TO MON. DE GUILBERT

I GIVE way to the desire of my heart, dearest! I love you. I feel as much pleasure and torture as if it were the first and the last times in my life that I pronounced these words. Ah! why do you torture me?—why am I so humbled? You will know some day. Alas! you will understand me. It is dreadful that I must always suffer for you, and through you. Is that for loving you? Adieu, dearest friend.

MDLLE DE LESPINASSE TO MON.
DE GUILBERT

DEAREST,

Upon returning home last night I found your letter. I did not expect this happiness; but what afflicts me is, that so many days must elapse before I can hope to see you. Ah, if you knew what sort of days these are, what life itself is, deprived of the interest and pleasure of seeing you! Dear friend, occupation, business and pleasure suffice you; but for me you are my only happiness, you only. I would not care to live but for the pleasure of seeing you, and of loving you every moment of my life. Let me hear from you. Adieu. I expect the letter you promised me.

In haste, yours ever.

JOHN KEATS TO FANNY BRAWNE
July 3, 1819.
Shanklin.

My Dearest Lady,

I am glad I had not an opportunity of sending off a letter which I wrote for you on Tuesday night—'twas too much like one out of Rousseau's 'Heloise.' I am more reasonable this morning. The morning is the only proper time for me to write to a beautiful girl whom I love so much; for at night, when the lonely day has closed, and the lonely, silent, unmusical chamber is waiting to receive me, as in a sepulchre, then, believe me, my passion gets entirely the sway. Then I would not have you see those rhapsodies which I once thought impossible I should ever give way to, and which I have often laughed at in another, for fear you should think me either too unhappy or a little mad. . . . Ask yourself, my love, whether you are not very cruel to have so entrammelled me, so destroyed my freedom? Will you confess this in the letter you must write immediately, and do all you can to console me in it—make it rich as a draught of poppies to intoxicate me, write the softest words and kiss them, that I may at least touch my lips where yours have been. For myself I know not how to express my devotion to so fair a form; I want a brighter word than bright, a fairer word than fair.

JOHN KEATS TO FANNY BRAWNE

My Sweet Girl,

Your letter gave me more delight than anything in the world but yourself could do; indeed, I am almost astonished that any absent one should have that luxurious power over my senses which I feel. Even when I am not thinking of you I receive your influence and I feel a tenderer nature stealing over me. All my thoughts, my unhappiest days and nights, have, I find, not cured me of my love of beauty, but made it so intense that I am miserable that you are not with me. . . I never knew before what such a love as you have made me feel was; I did not believe in it; my fancy was afraid of it, lest it should burn me up. But if you will fully love me, though there may be some fire, 'twill not be more than we can bear when moistened and bedewed with pleasure. . . . I would never see anything but pleasure in your eyes, love on your lips, and happiness in your steps. I would wish to see you among those amusements suitable to your inclinations and spirits; so that our loves might be a delight in the midst of pleasures agreeable enough, rather than a resource from vexations and cares.

JOHN KEATS TO FANNY BRAWNE

Sweetest Fanny,

You fear sometimes I do not love you so much as you wish. My dear girl, I love you ever and ever, and without reserve. The more I have known the more I have loved. In every way—even my jealousies have been agonies of love, in the hottest fit I ever had I would have died for you. I have vexed you too much. But for love! Can I help it? You are always new. The last of your kisses was ever the sweetest; the last smile the brightest; the last movement the gracefullest. When you passed my window home yesterday, I was filled with so much admiration as if I had then seen you for the first time. . . . Even if you did not love me I could not help an entire devotion to you; how much more deeply, then, must I feel for you, knowing you love me.

Sudden love is the latest cured.
 LA BRUYERE, *Les Caracteres*

He in a few minutes ravished this fair creature, or at least would have ravished her, if she had not, by a timely compliance, prevented him.
 HENRY FIELDING, *Jonathan Wilde*

Jupiter himself was turned into a satyr, a shepherd, a bull, a swan, a golden shower, and what not for love.
 ROBERT BURTON, *The Anatomy of Melancholy*

By heaven, I do love: and it hath taught me to rhyme, and to be melancholy.
 SHAKESPEARE, *Love's Labour's Lost*

THE NIGHT-PIECE, TO JULIA

Her Eyes the Glow-worm lend thee,
The Shooting Stars attend thee;
 And the Elves also,
 Whose little eyes glow,
Like the sparks of fire, befriend thee.

No Will-o'-the-Wisp mis-light thee;
Nor Snake, or Slow-worm bite thee:
 But on, on thy way
 Not making a stay,
Since Ghost there's none to affright thee.

Let not the dark thee cumber;
What though the Moon does slumber?
 The Stars of the night,
 Will lend thee their light,
Like tapers clear without number.

Then Julia let me woo thee,
Thus, thus to come unto me:
 And when I shall meet
 Thy silv'ry feet,
My soul I'll pour into thee.

      Robert Herrick

GIVE ALL TO LOVE

Give all to love;
Obey thy heart;
Friends, kindred, days,
Estate, good fame,
Plans, credit and the Muse, —
Nothing refuse.

'Tis a brave master;
Let it have scope:
Follow it utterly,
Hope beyond hope:
High and more high
It dives into noon,
With wing unspent,
Untold intent;
But it is a god,
Knows its own path
And the outlets of the sky.

It was never for the mean;
It requireth courage stout.
Souls above doubt,
Valour unbending,

It will reward,—
They shall return
More than they were,
And ever ascending.

Leave all for love;
Yet, hear me, yet,
One word more thy heart behoved,
One pulse more of firm endeavour,—
Keep thee today,
Tomorrow, forever,
Free as an Arab
Of thy beloved.

Cling with life to the maid;
But when the surprise,
First vague shadow of surmise
Flits across her bosom young,
Of a joy apart from thee,
Free be she, fancy-free;
Nor thou detain her vesture's hem,
Nor the palest rose she flung
From her summer diadem.

Though thou loved her as thyself,
As a self of purer clay,
Though her parting dims the day,
Stealing grace from all alive;
Heartily know,
When half-gods go,
The gods arrive.

Ralph Waldo Emerson

And by Love's sweetest part, Variety, she swore.

JOHN DONNE, *The Indifferent*

Alas! the love of women! it is known
To be a lovely and a fearful thing!

LORD BYRON, *Don Juan*

True love is like seeing ghosts: we all talk about it,
but few of us have ever seen one.
    LA ROCHEFOUCAULD

When a man talks of love, with caution trust him;
But if he swears, he'll certainly deceive thee.
    THOMAS OTWAY, *The Orphan*

He that would the daughter win,
Must with the mother first begin.
    JOHN RAY, *English Proverbs*

    And then the lover,
Sighing like a furnace, with a woeful ballad
Made to his mistress' eyebrow.
    SHAKESPEARE, *As You Like It*

ROBERT BURNS TO ELLISON
BEGBIE

I HAVE often thought it a peculiarly unlucky circumstance in love, that though in every other situation in life telling the truth is not only the safest, but actually by far the easiest way of proceeding, a lover is never under greater difficulty in acting, nor never more puzzled for expression than when his passion is sincere and his intentions honourable.

I do not think that it is very difficult for a person of ordinary capacity to talk of love and fondness which are not felt, and to make vows of constancy and fidelity which are never intended to be performed, if he be villain enough to practise such detestable conduct; but to a man whose heart glows with the principles of integrity and truth, and who sincerely loves a woman of amiable person, uncommon refinement of sentiment, and purity of manners, to such a one in such circumstances, I can assure you my dear, from my own feelings at this present moment, courtship is a task indeed. There is such a number of foreboding fears and distrustful anxieties crowd into my mind when I am in your company, or when I sit down to write to you, that what to speak or what to write I am altogether at a loss.

There is one rule which I have hitherto practised and which I shall invariably keep with you and that is, honestly to tell you the plain truth. There is something so mean and unmanly in the acts of dissimulation and falsehood that I am surprised they can be acted by any one in so noble, so generous a passion as virtuous love. No, my dear E., I shall never endeavour to gain your favour by such detestable practices. If you will be so good and so generous as to admit me for your partner, your companion, your bosom friend through life, there is nothing on this side of eternity shall give me greater transport: but I shall never think of purchasing your hand by any arts unworthy of a man, and, I will add, of a Christian.

There is one thing my dear, which I earnestly request of you and it is this that you should soon either put an end to my hopes by a peremptory refusal or cure me of my fears by a generous consent.

It would oblige me much if you would send me a line or two when convenient. I shall only add further that if a behaviour regulated (though perhaps but very imperfectly) by the rules of honour, and virtue of a heart devoted to love and esteem you, and an earnest endeavour to promote your happiness—if these are qualities you would wish in a friend, in a husband, I hope you shall ever find them in your real friend and sincere lover.

LORD BYRON TO COUNTESS GUICCIOLI

My Dearest Teresa,—I have read this book in your garden. My love, you were absent, or else I could not have read it. It is a favourite book of yours, and the writer was a friend of mine. You will not understand these English words, and *others* will not understand them, which is the reason I have not scrawled them in Italian. But you will recognise the handwriting of him who passionately loved you, and you will divine that, over a book which was yours, he could only think of love. In that word, beautiful in all languages, but most so in yours—*Amor moi*—is comprised my existence here and hereafter. I feel I exist here, and I fear that I shall exist hereafter—to what purpose you will decide; my destiny rests with you, and you are a woman, seventeen years of age, and two out of a convent. I wish that you had stayed there, with all my heart—or at least that I had never met you in your married state.

But all this is too late. I love you, and you love me—at least you *say so,* and *act* as if you *did* so, which last is a great consolation in all events. But I more than love you, and cannot cease to love you.

Think of me sometimes when the Alps and the ocean divide us—but they never will, unless you *wish* it.

BYRON.

Bologna,
Aug. 25, 1819.

Now sleeps the crimson petal, now the white;
Nor waves the cypress in the palace walk;
Nor winks the gold fin in the porphyry font:
The fire-fly wakens: waken thou with me.

Now droops the milk-white peacock like a ghost,
And like a ghost she glimmers on to me.

Now lies the Earth all Danae to the stars,
And all thy heart lies open unto me.
Now slides the silent meteor on, and leaves
A shining furrow, as thy thoughts in me.

Now folds the lily all her sweetness up,
And slips into the bosom of the lake:
So fold thyself, my dearest, thou, and slip
Into my bosom and be lost in me.

   ALFRED, LORD TENNYSON, *The Princess*

One should always be in love. That is the reason one
should never marry.
   OSCAR WILDE, *A Woman of No Importance,*

SHE WALKS IN BEAUTY

She walks in beauty, like the night
  Of cloudless climes and starry skies;
And all that's best of dark and bright
  Meet in her aspect and her eyes:
Thus mellowed to that tender light
  Which heaven to gaudy day denies.

One shade the more, one ray the less,
  Had half impaired the nameless grace
Which waves in every raven tress,
  Or softly lightens o'er her face;
Where thoughts serenely sweet express
  How pure, how dear their dwelling place.

And on that cheek, and o'er that brow,
  So soft, so calm, yet eloquent,
The smiles that win, the tints that glow,
  But tell of days in goodness spent,
A mind at peace with all below,
  A heart whose love is innocent!

Lord Byron

When we met first and loved, I did not build
Upon the vent with marble. Could it mean
To last, a love set pendulous between
Sorrow and sorrow? Nay, I rather thrilled,
Distrusting every light that seemed to gild
The onward path, and feared to overlean
A finger even. And, though I have grown serene
And strong since then, I think that God has willed
A still renewable fear . . . O love, O troth . . .
Lest these enclasped hands should never hold,
This mutual kiss drop down between us both
As an unowned thing, once the lips being cold.
And Love, be false! if he, to keep one oath,
Must lose one joy, by his life's star foretold.

Elizabeth Barrett Browning

I never gave a lock of hair away
To a man, Dearest, except this to thee,
Which now upon my fingers thoughtfully,
I ring out to the full brown length and say
'Take it'. My day of youth went yesterday;
My hair no longer bounds to my foot's glee,
Nor plant I it from rose or myrtle-tree,
As girls do, any more: it only may
Now shade on two pale cheeks the mark of tears,
Taught drooping from the head that hangs aside
Through sorrow's trick. I though the funeral-shears
Would take this first, but Love is justified -
Take it thou, - finding pure, from all those years,
The kiss my mother left here when she died.

Elizabeth Barrett Browning

I think of thee! - my thoughts do twine and bud
About thee, as wild vines, about a tree,
Put out broad leaves, and soon there's nought to see
Except the straggling green which hides the wood.
 Yet, O my palm tree, be it understood
I will not have my thoughts instead of thee
Who are dearer, better! Rather, instantly
Renew thy presence; as a strong tree should,
Rustle thy boughs and set thy trunk all bare,
And let these bands of greenery which insphere thee
Drop heavily down, - burst, shattered, everywhere!
Because, in this deep joy to see and hear thee
And breathe within thy shadow a new air,
I do not think of thee - I am too near thee.

Elizabeth Barrett Browning

If I leave all for thee, wilt thou exchange
And be all to me? Shall I never miss
Home-talk and blessing and the common kiss
That comes to each in turn, nor count it strange,
When I look up, to drop on a new range
Of walls and floors, another home than this?
Nay, wilt thou fill that place by me which is
Filled by dead eyes too tender to know change?
That's hardest. If to conquer love, has tried,
To conquer grief, tries more, as all things prove;
For grief indeed is love and grief beside.
Alas, I have grieved so I am hard to love.
Yet love me - wilt thou? Open thine heart wide,
And fold within the wet wings of thy dove.

Elizabeth Barrett Browning

WILLIAM HAZLITT TO SARAH
WALKER

YOU will scold me for this, and ask me if this is keeping my promise to mind my work. One half of it was to think of Sarah; and besides I do not neglect my work either I assure you. I regularly do ten pages a day, which mounts up to thirty guineas' worth a week, so that you see I should grow rich at this rate, if I could keep on so; *and I could keep on so,* if I had you with me to encourage me with your sweet smiles, and share my lot. The Berwick smacks sail twice a week, and the wind sets fair. When I think of the thousand endearing caresses that have passed between us, I do not wonder at the strong attachment that draws me to you, but I am sorry for my own want of power to please. I hear the wind sigh through the lattice and keep repeating over and over to myself two lines of Lord Byron's tragedy—

'So shalt thou find me ever at thy side,
Here and hereafter, if the last may be.'

applying them to thee, my love, and thinking whether I shall ever see thee again. Perhaps not—for some years at least—till both thou and I are old—and then when all else have forsaken thee, I will creep to thee, and die in thine arms.

You once made me believe I was not hated by her I loved: and for that sensation—so delicious was it, though but a mockery and a dream—I owe you more than I can ever pay. I thought to have dried up my tears for ever the day I left you: but as I write this they stream again. If they did not, I think my heart would burst.

I walk out here on an afternoon and hear the notes of the thrush that comes up from a sheltered valley below, welcome in the spring; but they do not melt my heart as they used; it is grown cold and dead. As you say it will one day be colder. God forgive what I have written above; I did not intend it; but you were once my little all, and I cannot bear the thought of having lost you forever, I fear through my own fault. Has any one called? Do not send any letters that come. I should like you and your mother (if agreeable) to go and see Mr Kean in 'Othello' and Miss Stephens in 'Love In A Village,' if you will, I will

write to Mr T ——— to send you tickets. Has Mr P ——
called? I think I must send to him for the picture to
kiss and talk to. Kiss me my best beloved. Ah! if you
can never be mine, still let me be your proud and
happy slave.

H.

THE PASSIONATE PILGRIM

Live with me, and be my love,
And we will all the pleasures prove
That hills and valleys, dales and fields,
And all the craggy mountains yields.

There will we sit upon the rocks,
And see the shepherds feed their flocks,
By shallow rivers, by whose falls
Melodious birds sing madrigals.

There will I make thee a bed of roses,
With a thousand fragrant posies,
A cap of flowers, and a kirtle
Embroidered all with leaves of myrtle;

A belt of straw and ivy buds,
With coral clasps and amber studs.
And if these pleasures may thee move,
Then live with me and be my love.

Love's Answer
If that the world and love were young,
And truth in every shepherd's tongue,
These pretty pleasures might me move,
To live with thee and by thy love.

William Shakespeare

WILLIAM CONGREVE TO
MRS. ARABELLA HUNT

NOT believe that I love you? You cannot pretend to be so incredulous. If you do not believe my tongue, consult my eyes, consult your own. You will find by yours that they have charms; by mine that I have a heart which feels them. Recall to mind what happened last night. That at least was a lover's kiss. Its eagerness, its fierceness, its warmth expressed the god its parent. But oh! its sweetness, and its melting softness expressed him more. With trembling in my limbs, and fevers in my soul, I ravished it. Convulsions, pantings, murmurings shew'd the mighty disorder within me: the mighty disorder increased by it. For those dear lips shot through my heart, and through my bleeding vitals, delicious poison, and an avoidless but yet charming ruin. What cannot a day produce? The night before I thought myself a happy man, in want of nothing, and in fairest expectation of fortune; approved of by men of wit, and applauded by others. Pleased, nay charmed with my friends, my then dearest friends, sensible of every delicate pleasure, and in their turns possessing all. But Love, almighty Love, seems in a moment to have removed me to a prodigious distance from every object but you alone. In the midst of crowds I remain in solitude. Nothing but you can lay hold of my mind, and that can lay hold of nothing but you. I appear transported to some foreign desert with you (oh, that I were really thus transported!) where, abundantly supplied with everything, in thee, I might live out an age of uninterrupted ecstasy. The scene of the world's great stage seems suddenly and sadly changed. Unlovely objects all around me, excepting thee; the charms of all the world appear to be translated to thee. Thus in this sad, but ah, too pleasing state! my soul can fix upon nothing but thee; thee it contemplates, admires, adores, nay depends on, trusts on you alone. If you and hope forsake it, despair and endless misery attend it.

Is it indeed so? If I lay here dead,
Wouldst thou miss any life in losing mine?
And would the sun for thee more coldly shine
Because of grave-damps falling round my head?
I marvelled, my Beloved, when I read
Thy thought so in the letter. I am thine -
But . . . so much to thee? Can I pour thy wine
While my hands tremble? Then my soul, instead
Of dreams of death, resumes life's lower range.
Then love me, Love! look on me - breathe on me!
As brighter ladies do not count it strange,
For love, to give up acres and degree,
I yield the grave for thy sake, and exchange
My near sweet view of Heaven, for earth with thee!

Elizabeth Barrett Browning

I lived with visions for my company
Instead of men and women, years ago,
And found them gentle mates, nor thought to know
A sweeter music than they played to me.
But soon their trailing purple was not free
Of this world's dust, their lutes did silent grow,
And I myself grew faint and blind below
Their vanishing eyes. Then THOU didst come - to be,
Beloved, what they seemed. Their shining fronts,
Their songs, their splendours (better, yet the same,
As river-water hallowed into fonts),
Met in thee, and from out thee overcame
My soul with satisfaction of all wants:
Because God's gifts put man's best dreams to shame.

Elizabeth Barrett Browning

NATHANIEL HAWTHORNE TO
HIS WIFE

I DO trust, my dearest, that you have been employing this bright day for both of us; for I have spent it in my dungeon, and the only light that broke upon me was when I opened your letter. I am sometimes driven to wish that you and I could mount upon a cloud (as we used to fancy in those heavenly walks of ours), and be borne quite out of sight and hearing of the world; for now all the people in the world seem to come between us. How happy were Adam and Eve! There was no third person to come between them, and all the infinity around them only seemed to press their hearts closer together. We love one another as well as they; but there is no silent and lovely garden of Eden for us. Will you sail away with me to discover some summer island? Do you not think that God has reserved one for us, ever since the beginning of the world? Foolish that I am to raise a question of it, since we have found such an Eden—such an island sacred to us two—whenever we have been together! Then we are the Adam and Eve of a virgin earth.

Now, good-bye; for voices are babbling around me and I should not wonder if you were to hear the echo of them while you read this letter.

LAURENCE STERNE TO MISS L.

YES! I will steal from the world, and not a babbling tongue shall tell where I am. Echo shall not so much as whisper my hiding-place. Suffer thy imagination to permit it as a little sun-gilt cottage, on the side of a romantic hill. Dost thou think 1 will leave love and friendship behind me? No! they shall be my companions in solitude, for they will sit down and rise up with me in the amiable form of my L———. We will be as merry and as innocent as our first parents in Paradise, before the arch-fiend entered that indescribable scene.

The kindest affections will have room to shoot and expand in our retirement, and produce such fruit as madness and envy and ambition have always killed in the bud. Let the human tempest and hurricane rage at a distance, the desolation is beyond the horizon of peace. My L——— has seen a polyanthus blow in December—some friendly wall has sheltered it from the biting wind. No planetary influence shall reach us but that which presides and cherishes the sweetest flowers. God preserve us! How delightful this prospect in idea! We will build and we will plant in our own way—simplicity shall not be tortured by art. We will learn of nature how to live—she shall be our alchemist, to mingle all the good of life in one salubrious draught. The gloomy family of care and distrust shall be banished from our dwelling, guarded by the kind and tutelar deity. We will sing our choral songs of gratitude and rejoice to the end of our pilgrimage.

Adieu, my L———

Return to one who languishes for your society.

L. STERNE.

CHARLOTTE CARPENTER TO
SIR WALTER SCOTT

IF I could but really believe that my letter only gave you half the pleasure you express, I almost think, my dearest Scott, that I should get very fond of writing, just to indulge you,—that is saying a great deal. I hope you are sensible of the compliment I pay you, and don't expect I shall always be so pretty behaved. You may depend on. me, my dearest friend, for fixing as *early* a day as I possibly can, and if it happens not to be so soon as you could wish, you must not be angry with me. It is very unlucky you are such a bad house-keeper, as I am no better. I shall try. I hope very soon to have the pleasure of seeing you, and of telling you how much I love you; but I wish the first fortnight was over. With all my love, and all sorts of pretty things, Adieu.

CHARLOTTE.

P.S. Etudiez votre Français. Remember you are to teach me Italian in return, but I shall be a stupid scholar.

Shall I compare thee to a Summer's day?
Thou art more lovely and more temperate:
Rough winds do shake the darling buds of May,
And Summer's lease hath all too short a date:
Sometime too hot the eye of heaven shines,
And often is his gold complexion dimm'd,
And every fair from fair sometime declines,
By chance, or natures changing course untrim'd:
But thy eternal Summer shall not fade,
Nor loose possession of that fair thou ow'st,
Nor shall death brag thou wandr'st in his shade,
When in eternal lines to time thou grow'st,
    So long as men can breathe or eyes can see,
    So long lives this, and this gives life to thee.

                        William Shakespeare

Woman begins by resisting a man's advances and ends
by blocking his retreat.

                    OSCAR WILDE

Beloved, thou has brought me many flowers
Plucked in the garden, all the summer through
And winter, and it seemed as if they grew
In this close room, nor missed the sun and showers.
So, in the like name of that love of ours,
Take back these thoughts which here unfolded too,
And which on warm and cold days I withdrew
From my heart's ground. Indeed, those beds and bowers
Be overgrown with bitter weeds and rue,
And wait thy weeding; yet here's eglantine,
Here's ivy! - take them, as I used to do
Thy flowers, and keep them where they shall not pine.
Instruct thine eyes to keep their colours true,
And tell thy soul their roots are left in mine.

Elizabeth Barrett Browning

And yet, because thou overcomest so,
Because thou are more noble and like a king,
Thou canst prevail against my fears and fling
Thy purple round me, till my heart shall grow
Too close against thine heart henceforth to know
How it shook when alone. Why, conquering
May prove as lordly and complete a thing
In lifting upward, as in crushing low!
And as a vanquished soldier yields his sword
To one who lifts him from the bloody earth,
Even so, Beloved, I at last record,
Here ends my strife. If <u>thou</u> invite me forth,
I rise above abasement at the word.
Make thy love larger to enlarge my worth.

Elizabeth Barrett Browning

Say over again, and yet once over again,
That thou dost love me. Though the word repeated
Should seem a 'cuckoo-song', as thou dost treat it,
Remember, never to the hill or plain,
Valley and wood, without her cuckoo-strain
Comes the fresh Spring in all her green completed.
Beloved, I, amid the darkness greeted
By a doubtful spirit-voice, in that doubt's pain
Cry, 'Speak once more - thou lovest!' Who can fear
Too many stars, though each in heaven shall roll,
Too many flowers, though each shall crown the year?
Say thou dost love me, love me, love me - toll
The silver iterance! - only minding, Dear,
To love me also in silence with thy soul.

Elizabeth Barrett Browning

THE ECSTASY

Where, like a pillow on a bed,
  A pregnant bank swelled up, to rest
The violet's reclining head,
  Sat we two, one anothers best.
Our hands were firmly cemented
  With a fast balm, which thence did spring,
Our eye-beams twisted, and did thread
  Our eyes, upon one double string;
So to entergraft our hands, as yet
  Was all the means to make us one,
And pictures in our eyes to get
  Was all our propagation.
As 'twixt two equal armies, Fate
  Suspends uncertain victory,
Our souls, (which to advance their state,
  Were gone out,) hung 'twixt her, and me.
And whil'st our souls negotiate there,
  We like sepulchral statues lay;
All day, the same our postures were,
  And we said nothing, all the day.
If any, so by love refin'd,
  That he souls language understood,
And by good love were grown all mind,

Within convenient distance stood,
He (though he knew not which soul spake,
  Because both meant, both spake the same)
Might thence a new concoction take,
  And part far purer than he came.
This Ecstasy doth unperplex
  (We said) and tell us what we love,
We see by this, it was not sex,
  We see, we saw not what did move:
But as all several souls contain
  Mixture of things, they know not what,
Love, these mixed souls, doth mix again,
  And makes both one, each this and that.
A single violet transplant,
  The strength, the colour, and the size,
(All which before was poor, and scant,)
  Redoubles still, and multiplies.
When love, with one another so
  Interinanimates two souls,
That abler soul, which thence doth flow,
  Defects of loneliness controls.
We then, who are this new soul, know,
  Of what we are compos'd, and made,

For, th'Atomies of which we grow,
    Are souls whom no change can invade.
But O alas, so long, so far
    Our bodies why do we forbear?
They are ours, though they are not we, We are
    The intelligences, they the spheres.
We owe them thanks, because they thus,
    Did us, to us, at first convey,
Yielded their forces, sense, to us,
    Nor are dross to us, but alloy.
On man heaven's influence works not so,
    But that it first imprints the air,
So soul into the soul may flow,
    Though it to body first repair.
As our blood labours to beget
    Spirits, as like souls as it can,
Because such fingers need to knit
    That subtle knot, which makes us man:
So must pure lovers' souls descend
    T'affections, and to faculties,
Which sense may reach and apprehend,
    Else a great Prince in prison lies.
To our bodies turn we then, that so

Weak men on love reveal'd may look;
Loves mysteries in souls do grow,
But yet the body is his book.
And if some lover, such as we,
Have heard this dialogue of one,
Let him still mark us, he shall see
Small change, when we're to bodies gone.

John Donne

NAPOLEON TO JOSEPHINE
Marmirolo.

I HAVE your letter my adorable love. It has filled my heart with joy. . . . Since I left you I have been sad all the time. My only happiness is near you. I go over endlessly in my thought your kisses, your tears, your delicious jealousy. The charm of my wonderful Josphine kindles a living blazing fire in my heart and senses. When shall I be able to pass every minute near you, with nothing to do but to love you and nothing to think of but the pleasure of telling you of it and giving you proof of it? I fancied that I loved you some time ago; but since then I feel that I love you a thousand times better. Ever since I have known you I adore you more every day. That proves how wrong is that saying of La Bruyère 'Love comes all of a sudden.' Ah, let me see some of your faults; be less beautiful, less graceful, less tender, less good. But never be jealous and never shed tears. Your tears send me out of my mind—they set my very blood on fire. Believe me that it is utterly impossible for me to have a single thought that is not yours, a single fancy that is not submissive to your will. Rest well. Restore your health. Come back to me and then at any rate before we die we ought to be able to say: 'We were happy for so very many days!' Millions of kisses, even to your dog.

JOSEPHINE TO NAPOLEON
Navarre, 1810.

A THOUSAND, thousand, tender thanks that you have not forgotten me. My son has just brought me your letter. With what eagerness have I read it; and yet it required much time, for there was not one word in it which did not make me weep. But these tears were very sweet. I have recovered my heart all entire, and such as it will ever remain. These are sentiments which are even life, and which can only pass away with life. I am in despair that my letter of the 19th has wounded you. I can not recall entirely the expressions, but I know the very painful sentiment which dictated it. It was that of chagrin in not hearing from you. I had written to you at my departure from Malmaison, and since, how many times have I desired to write to you! But I perceived the reason of your silence, and I feared to be obtrusive by a letter. Yours has been a balm to me. May you be happy; may you be as happy as you deserve to be. It is my heart all entire which speaks to you. You have just given me my happiness, and a portion most sensibly appreciated. Nothing can be more precious to me than a token of your remembrance. Adieu, my love. I thank you as tenderly as I always love you.

Josephine.

VANESSA TO SWIFT

YOU bid me be easy and you would see me as often as you could. You had better have said, as often as you could get the better of your inclinations so much, or as often as you remember there was such a one in the world. If you continue to treat me as you do, you will not be made uneasy by me long. It is impossible to describe what I have suffered since I saw you last. I am sure I could have borne the rack much better than those killing, killing words of yours. Sometimes I have resolved to die without seeing you more, but those resolves, to your misfortune, did not last long. For there is something in human nature that prompts one so to find relief in this world. I must give way to it, and beg you would see me, and speak kindly to me; for I am sure you would not condemn anyone to suffer what I have done, could you but know it. The reason I write to you is, because I cannot tell it to you should I see you; for when I begin to complain, then you are angry, and there is something in your looks so awful, that it strikes me dumb. O! but that you may have but so much regard for me left, that this complaint may touch your soul with pity! I say as little as I can; did you but know what I thought, I am sure it would move you to forgive me: and believe I cannot help telling you this and live.

It is as absurd to deny that it is possible for a man always to love the same woman, as it would be to affirm that some famous musician needed several violins in order to execute a piece of music or compose a charming melody.

HONORE DE BALZAC, *The Physiology of Marriage*

Anything may be expected and anything may be supposed of a woman who is in love.

HONORE DE BALZAC, *The Physiology of Marriage*

To speak of love is to make love.

HONORE DE BALZAC, *The Physiology of Marriage*

To enlarge or illustrate this power and effect of love is to set a candle in the sun.

ROBERT BURTON, *The Anatomy of Melancholy*

In her first passion woman loves her lover;
In all the others, all she loves is love.

LORD BYRON, *Don Juan*

Blessed is the wooing that is not long adoing.

ROBERT BURTON, *The Anatomy of Melancholy*

Love comes in at the window and goes out at the door.

WILLIAM CAMDEN, *Remains*

Religion has done love a great service by making it a sin.

ANATOLE FRANCE

TO:

One word is too often profaned
For me to profane it;
One feeling too falsely disdain'd
For thee to disdain it;
One hope is too like despair
For prudence to smother;
And pity from thee more dear
Than that from another.

I can give not what men call love:
But wilt thou accept not
The worship the heart lifts above
And the heavens reject not,
The desire of the moth for the star,
Of the night for the morrow,
The devotion to something afar
From the sphere of our sorrow?

Percy Bysshe Shelley

MY TRUE LOVE HATH MY HEART

My true love hath my heart, and I have his,
By just exchange, one for the other given.
I hold his dear, and mine he cannot miss:
There never was a better bargain driven.

His heart in me, keeps me and him in one,
My heart in him, his thoughts and senses guides:
He loves my heart, for once it was his own:
I cherish his, because in me it bides.

His heart his wound received from my sight:
My heart was wounded, with his wounded heart,
For as from me, on him his hurt did light,
So still me thought in me his hurt did smart:
*   Both equal hurt, in this change sought our bliss:*
*   My true love hath my heart and I have his.*

Sir Philip Sidney

'Tis well to be merry and wise,
'Tis well to be honest and true;
'Tis well to be off with the old love,
Before you are on with the new.

MATURIN, *Bertram. Motto.*

RONDEAU

Jenny kissed me when we met,
    Jumping from the chair she sat in;
Time, you thief, who love to get
    Sweets into your list, put that in!
Say I'm weary, say I'm sad
    Say that health and wealth have missed me,
Say I'm growing old, but add,
      Jenny kissed me.

Leigh Hunt

He sees her coming, and begins to glow
Even as a dying coal revives with wind,
And with his bonnet hides his angry brow,
Looks on the dull earth with disturbed mind,
 Taking no notice that she is so nigh,
 For all askance he holds her in his eye.

O what a sight it was, wistly to view
How she came stealing to the wayward boy!
To note the fighting conflict of her hue!
How white and red each other did destroy!
 But now her cheek was pale, and by and by
 It flash'd forth fire, as lightning fromtthe sky.

Now was she just before him as he sat,
And like a lowly lover down she kneels;
With one fair hand she heaveth up his hat,
Her other tender hand his fair cheek feels;
 His tend'rer cheek receives her soft hand's print
 As apt as new-fall'n snow takes any dint.

O, what a war of looks was then between them,
Her eyes, petitioners, to his eyes suing!
His eyes saw her eyes as they had not seen them;
Her eyes wooed still, his eyes disdain'd the wooing;
    And all this dumb play had his acts made plain
    With tears which chorus-like her eyes did rain.

Full gently now she takes him by the hand,
A lily prison'd in a gaol of snow,
Or ivory in an alabaster band;
So white a friend engirts so white a foe.
    This beauteous combat, wilful and unwilling,
    Showed like two silver doves that sit a-billing.

William Shakespeare, from *Venus and Adonis*

KLOPSTOCK TO META, HIS WIFE

WITH what transport do I think of you, my Meta, my only treasure, my wife!

When I fancy I behold you, my mind is filled with the heavenly thoughts which so often fervently and delightfully occupy it; and while I think of you they are still more fervent, more delightful. They glow in my breast but no words can express them. You are dearer to me than all who are connected with me by blood or by friendship, dearer than all which is dearer to me besides in creation. My sister, my friend, you are mine by love, by pure and holy love, which Providence (O how grateful am I for the blessing) has made the inhabitant of my soul on earth. It appears to me that you were born my twin sister in Paradise. At present, indeed, we are not there, but we shall return thither. Since we have so much happiness here, what shall we have there?

Remember me to all our friends. My Meta, my for ever beloved, I am entirely yours.

I love to be envied, and would not marry a wife that I alone could love; loving alone is as dull as eating alone.

WYCHERLEY, *The Country Wife,*

*Let me not to the marriage of true minds
Admit impediments, love is not love
Which alters when it alteration finds,
Or bends with the remover to remove.
O no, it is an ever fixed mark
That looks on tempests and is never shaken;
It is the star to every wandering bark,
Whose worth's unknown, although his height be taken.
Love's not Time's fool, though rosy lips and cheeks
Within his bending sickles compass come,
Love alters not with his brief hours and weeks,
But bears it out even to the edge of doom:*
    If this be error and upon me proved,
    I never writ, nor no man ever loved.

William Shakespeare

SONG: TO CELIA

Drink to me, only, with thine eyes,
*   And I will pledge with mine;*
Or leave a kiss but in the cup,
*   And I'll not look for wine.*
The thirst, that from the soul does rise,
*   Does ask a drink divine:*
But might I of Jove's Nectar sup,
*   I would not change for thine.*
I sent thee, late, a rose wreath,
*   Not so much honouring thee,*
As giving it a hope, that there
*   It could not withered be.*
But thou thereon did'st only breathe.
*   And sent it back to me:*
Since when it grows, and smells, I swear,
*   Not of itself, but thee.*

Ben Jonson

FALSE THOUGH SHE BE

False though she be to me and love,
I'll ne'er pursue revenge;
For still the charmer I approve,
Though I deplore her change.
In hours of bliss we oft have met:
They could not always last;
And though the present I regret,
I'm grateful for the past.

William Congreve

"UNLIKE ARE WE . . ."

Unlike are we, unlike, O princely Heart!
    Unlike our uses, and our destinies.
    Our ministering two angels look surprise
On one another, as they strike athwart
Their wings in passing. Thou, bethink thee, art
    A guest for queens to social pageantries,
    With gages from a hundred brighter eyes
Than tears even can make mine, to ply thy part
Of chief musician. What hast thou to do
    With looking from the lattice-lights at me,
A poor, tired, wandering singer?—singing through
    The dark, and leaning up a cypress tree?
The chrism is on thine head,—on mine the dew,—
    And Death must dig the level where these agree.

Elizabeth Barrett Browning

"IF THOU MUST LOVE ME . . ."

If thou must love me, let it be for nought
   Except for love's sake only. Do not say,
   "I love her for her smile—her look—her way
Of speaking gently—for a trick of thought
That falls in well with mine, and certes brought
   A sense of pleasant ease on such a day"—
   For these things in themselves, Beloved, may
Be changed, or change for thee,—and love, so wrought,
May be unwrought so. Neither love me for
   Thine own dear pity's wiping my cheeks dry,—
A creature might forget to weep, who bore
   Thy comfort long, and lose thy love thereby!
But love me for love's sake, that evermore
   Thou may'st love on, through love's eternity.

Elizabeth Barrett Browning

117

A RED, RED ROSE

Oh my love is like a red, red rose,
*   That's newly sprung in June:*
Oh my love is like the melodie,
*   That's sweetly play'd in tune.*

As fair art thou, my bonnie lass,
*   So deep in love am I;*
And I will love thee still, my dear,
*   Till a' the seas gang dry.*

Till a' the seas gang dry, my dear,
*   And the rocks melt wi' the sun;*
And I will love thee still, my dear,
*   While the sands o' life shall run.*

And fare thee well, my only love!
*   And fare thee well a while!*
And I will come again, my love,
*   Tho' it were ten thousand mile!*

Robert Burns

Young men want to be faithful and are not; old men want to be faithless and are not.

OSCAR WILDE, *The Picture of Dorian Gray.*

Nobody loves me; I'm going into the garden and eat worms.

UNKNOWN. *A Valentine Greeting.*

If men did not put their responsibilities above everything else, the bulk of love-making would not be done at night.

UNKNOWN, *Meditations in Wall Street.*

I dare not ask a kiss;
I dare not beg a smile;
Lest having that, or this,
I might grow proud the while.

No, no, the utmost share
Of my desire, shall be
Only to kiss that air,
That lately kissed thee.

ROBERT HERRICK, *To Electra.*

Give me a kiss, and to that kiss a score;
Then to that twenty, add a hundred more:
A thousand to that hundred: so kiss on,
To make that thousand up a million.
Treble that million, and when that is done,
Let's kiss afresh, as when we first begun.

ROBERT HERRICK, *To Anthea: Ah, My Anthea!*